CSU Poetry Series XXV

Trish Reeves

RETURNING THE QUESTION

Cleveland State University Poetry Center

ACKNOWLEDGMENTS

With gratitude to Joan Aleshire, Kenny Damacion, Stephen Dobyn, Dee Fonville, Virginia Frazier, Louise Glück, Joseph K. Houts, Sr., Patrici C. Houts, Noreen Houts, Joe Houts, Jr., Marilyn Hutchinson, Jennie Johnson, Kate Johnson, Robert C. Jones, Louise Kimberlin, Tom Lux, Sylvia Moss, Caroline Reeves, Jeremiah Reeves, Biff Russ, Ellen Voigt, and the Corporation of Yaddo.

Grateful acknowledgment is made to the editors of the following publications for poems that originally appeared in them:

IRONWOOD: "Guisborough Shore," "If I Believed in God," "Motion," "Short Memories"
MISSOURI POETS: AN ANTHOLOGY: "Alive" (in a slightly different version)
NEW LETTERS: "A Thought Remembered Is a Thought Forgotten," "Freedom"
PEQUOD: "I Say, Not Here, Not There, So Where?", "Watching," "When I Awakened Out of My Head," "Window"
PLOUGHSHARES: "And Then," "Goodbye," "Passion," "Rural Childhood," "The Silver Coin"
THE PLOUGHSHARES POETRY READER: "The Silver Coin"
POET & CRITIC: "Broken Ground"
PRAIRIE SCHOONER: "Cold Wind," "The Shawl Pin"
QUARTERLY WEST: "Infidelity," "Collect Calls"
SENECA REVIEW: "After Nature," "Driving Through," "Gathering My Parents," "Pure and Rapid," "Secret Communication"

Copyright © 1988 by Trish Reeves

ISBN 0-914946-67-6
   0-914946-66-8 (paperback)

Library of Congress Catalog Card Number: 88-7136

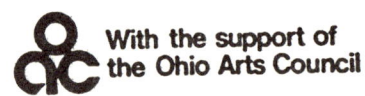

For Jerry

CONTENTS

I

Guisborough Shore   11
Tracery   12
Broken Ground   13
Goodbye   14
At the Royal Governor's Palace, Williamsburg   16
No Surprise in Springfield, Illinois   17
The Dark Window   18
The Circular Stroke   19
Infidelity   20
Collect Calls   21
Short Memories   22
A Thought Remembered Is a Thought Forgotten   23
I Say, Not Here, Not There, So Where?   24
If I Believed in God   26

II

Driving Through   29
Gathering   30
Pure and Rapid   31
Secret Communication   32
Window   33
Passion   35
And Then   37
When I Awakened Out of My Head   38
What We Don't Understand About Living   39
Watching   40
Dry   41
My Parents   42
Rural Childhood   43
How Life Came to the Land   44
Cold Wind   45

III

Death 49
Lucas Cranach 50
With, Without 51
The Shawl Pin 52
Light Plus Perspective 53
Alive 54
From the Studio 55
Freedom 57
After Nature 58
Long Step into Darkness 60
Motion 61
The Silver Coin 62

I

GUISBOROUGH SHORE

> *Turner's title merely means: drawings done on the shore while staying at Guisborough.*
> —Gerald Wilkinson

Brushing in the trees
rather than breathing them in:
this is life. Always a little more
water, and a little higher
water in the background. With notes
above the mountains and the clouds.
What does it mean
that Turner's mother was mad,
that the Royal Academy named him
Professor of Perspective,
that the professor's favorite word
after "light" was "doubt"?
It means nothing.
It means the world is made out of paint:
that the woman in the museum
who studies the blue wash of genius,
the paper with the crease down the center,
wishes to refold the sea,
take it home
and keep it in her heart, her storm.

TRACERY

Tracery did not begin as ornament.

You might say the open spaces
would not be so important
without the tracery: bars and bands
of stone and lead dividing the openings
or standing against the walls for pattern.

Tracery came from the night.
From the terror that stretched across the body
when the artist awakened to hear
his lover speak in her sleep
words so deeply sexual
that he knew they were meant
for someone else
or no one.

Everything the artist heard that night
he fashioned
into the first rose window.

BROKEN GROUND

I went to the wedding
and was married there.
Being the bride, I wore a necklace
of oysters. In my family
we eat the pearls
and string the animals.
We admire the way they lie
upon flesh, the way the juice
turns any white dress dark.
We call this a ceremony
of blameless touches. Sea flesh upon land
flesh bringing emotion innocently
the way color causes pain:
a certain green now unbearable
because the groom once wore a whole shirt of it.

GOODBYE

There was no air
and then there was nothing else
but air. This is called the filling
of the lungs for the first time.
The irreversible reverse
of this is when my mother calls me
and says: The flame fell off the candle
just like that.
And I say, Just like what?
And she says, I'm dead,
don't you hear me?

Of course I don't hear her.
I'm ten years old and riding
in my friend's convertible.
We're laughing at her mother
who is singing with the radio;
top down, no scarf, just singing
and every so often turning to the back seat
to give us a grin.

My old friend called and said,
My mother died.   Didn't you hear me?
Of course I heard her.
I'm thirty-six years old.
I'm back in the fifth grade
on one of those Mondays
when the words were whispered:
Your friend's mother
did it again—jumped up on a table
at the Country Club Saturday night
and sang the blues. What do you think
your friend thinks about that?

I thought maybe she didn't know.
Not everyone's parents told them
about those party stoppers.
Although mine told me,
I was still so young
I thought the blues must be something
you sang when you were happy.

AT THE ROYAL GOVERNOR'S PALACE, WILLIAMSBURG

Behind the chandeliers and portraits
wrapped in tulle (hot summertime),
beyond the blinding white walk
of broken shells, and even beyond
the gates of twisted initials,
the maze waits for the children of citizens.

O Governor, the holly still grows
sharp points in the labyrinth. My children
run back and forth from one dead end
to another. And I warn them
that their faces flush in the August air.

These children laugh.
They think they reach the center
of your formal dirt path.

Governor, the leaves of holly
grow so large,
and my children's faces so red
your confusion again blooms with berries.

NO SURPRISE IN SPRINGFIELD, ILLINOIS

Mary Lincoln's house is being shaken apart
by half-a-million people a year
walking through, walking through.
Mary Lincoln's government is studying
her house from the inside
like a constructive tourist
who wants to know more.
Too bad Mary isn't around to tell
the survey team the exact point
in the upstairs bedroom where she saw
her whole house shake apart stick by stick
the night Eddie died. The horse hair on the parlor
sofas and rockers already tinted black
in preparation for anything
but happiness.

THE DARK WINDOW

My shadow is so hungry
it's started feeding on me.
After kicking it away all day long
I have to sleep in complete absence of light
because lying down next to my shadow
is the most dangerous position I can take.

I have trouble sleeping.
Not because of my mother or father
or anyone I want or don't want.
But because of the darkness shifting around
in the spaces that float my brain in my head.
The darkness that, with the slightest amount
of light, slips out through my eyes
and becomes my shape,
a shape in black—the way the blind
know shape.

THE CIRCULAR STROKE

I see a sameness
in the egg
of yesterday and today.
The egg sitting there
with its hands in its pockets
—unfertilized, fertilized—
hands still in pockets
the egg is a cold lover
that begins
its lopsided roll
to say:
All is conflict
all is sex
all is a round rock
but for me.

INFIDELITY

I would like to see the sea spilling
into space—that means off the planet
not just into air—if you could be in that water
shouting, It's for sure, there's no such thing
as eternity. Then I would know that right to the end
you hadn't changed, that you still knew how
to bring the doubt from my throat
with your sureness. I would understand
your implication that we wouldn't have to
stay together forever, just a little longer.
      As wife and husband, we've earned a rest.

The woodwork's crazy because the moon's on it
tonight. We had some drinks, undressed
and then I saw the woodwork with a shine
that moved when the trees interfered with the moon.
This makes the woodwork crazy.
      Timing our time away from each other
      is difficult. One of us never wants to separate
      our vacations the same season.

The next house won't have any woodwork.
That way when the moon shines the woodwork
won't. I will keep my mind on undressing.
I will not turn from wood to the moon
and wonder, If the moon starts to fall
how long will it take to reach earth.
      I will not cry out for help
      while we're making love.

COLLECT CALLS

I become one of those people I've overheard
making calls from pay phones:
a woman untwisting the cord with her fingers.
She sometimes cries and
even though I'm not crying, I am
the woman on the phone
and the line feeds to a dark kitchen
below sleeping children
where a man whispers: I kicked in the bedroom
television tonight because the woman I love
most of all after you
plans to leave town. Call me
sick enough to hurt myself, he says.

I tell him to please speak up,
I know he's strong enough for this.
I untangle my right hand from the cord
and reach to finger the holes
in the dial. I'm standing in a corner
of a kitchen full of people at a party.
I know these people,
I know they're trying not to listen.
But the only form I see is his—
straight through the receiver,
a man framed by a black circle.

SHORT MEMORIES

In the first woodcut of the series
a man and a woman are waking up
with their necks badly bruised.
The huge bruises bleed onto their chests.
They wonder what they could have done in the night
to have caused this.

In the second block they sit in bed
and look in the mirror at their perfect necks.
The woman says: I dreamed my neck was bruised,
I could probably use more help than I get.
The man is angry and says like Martin Luther:
"All we do is in vain, even in the best life."

Can landscape stand alone? says the third woodcut.
It shows the man and woman now out of bed
leading naked people to the garden. Lowering torches
they clip hedges, flowers and trees with fire.
The animal painter Coignard sits on a bench and laughs
as he reaches for his sketch book.

Next print: naked vines.
This view is full of voices—
voices fill the spaces
between rough twisting vines.
The voices are old
and have the smooth incoherence of a dream.

The final cut is full of slipped strokes
on foreheads, thighs; unfortunate details
recalling black shapes from scraps of sleep
as the man and woman lie down for the night
under the title *What sustains a vault?*
Short wings.

A THOUGHT REMEMBERED IS A THOUGHT FORGOTTEN

Then there were fires
with people around them.
People who did not write anything down.
They thought the mind was sleep,
that white cloudy substance
so dearly loved by death.

An intrusion upon the mind was called wakefulness
and distinguished
by wide-eyed periods of confusion.

A return to the mind while standing—
called standing sleep—
was noticed on days after
one stayed up all night with a lover.

Wakefulness and death often fought
for the mind, but this was never written down.
Until people grew to tell themselves
from plants in this way:
When the tree loses a leaf in autumn
the new one it receives in spring
is not the same; when the lover loses
her wakefulness
it returns as the same wakefulness.

I SAY, NOT HERE, NOT THERE, SO WHERE?

Today I went back to where Jesse James used to live,
where he died. It's like a shrine in this town,
a shrine no one knows about or goes to
except me. It's a vacant lot.
But God what a view. On good days I get out of the car
and walk to the edge that drops sixty feet
at the back. I can see why he chose this ground
—it's a lookout—he could see the river,
and if he felt like it, he could look on into Kansas
where everything goes flat.
He could say, What's wrong with my life
is what's wrong with Kansas:
it just isn't worth a fuck.

Today I called an old friend.
I said, I clocked it in the car,
do you realize you grew up ten minutes
from the land on which Jesse James lived and died?
Our parents are a lot alike. Yours probably took you
to his house, as mine did. They probably
told you, This is the real thing, dear.
And my friend said, I don't know how you do it,
how you live here
without having been in the loony bin at least once.
My friend says she would leave tomorrow
but she can't get a flight.

On bad days I don't get out of the car at the vacant lot.
I didn't get out today.
I didn't even stop.
I'd already called two friends long distance,
been fortunate enough to receive one call
from a friend in town,

and then, as always on Mondays and Fridays,
I had driven eighty miles to sit in a doctor's office
for 46 minutes, and then driven another eighty miles home,
driving by the old James place on my return trip.

When I got home my children were smiling,
and the way we were interacting
indicated I was doing a decent job with them.
I hadn't felt this way for days.
And the night before
my husband and I made love in the way
people who love each other should make love.
I thought of all this in the middle of pain—
these good things, which do not make me stop hurting
on a day when I cry in the doctor's office
that I cannot grieve
for what was never mine to lose;
on a day when I am certain
the only thing keeping me alive is reluctance.

The part about Jesse James is in here because it's true.
It's my way of pulling a happy poem out of my gut
when it isn't there.

IF I BELIEVED IN GOD

I would paint a black horse
with red trappings, gold buckled
into the leather. I could paint the same horse
labeled green, or a white one called
Inverse Silhouette.
The white one would have silver clasps
and where I would normally
paint holes for the tongues of the buckles
I would paint eyes
alternating blue and brown eyes.
It would be life and death to mount
these horses that were always the same
but what a horse
with tongues in its eyes
and steel restraint in its mouth.

II

DRIVING THROUGH

When the riverbluffs were cut open
for a road and I started driving through
in the back seat of my parents' car
I began feeling like a river.
Rivers touch things—
tree roots, silver fish hooks
and fast fish—in such a way
that they feel nothing.

I was a river everywhere I went
on the farm. The small house
where my great-grandfather shook
his tobacco can of coins
and seemed about dead,
the back pond where the sounds of
high grass and rattlesnakes
imitated each other.
And the field where I saw
a coyote is greyer than the sky.

In the big house where I lived
I was a river, but not so brave.
If my mother bled from a razor cut
I almost cried. Also, if she and my father
fought, if my father didn't come home,
if my grandmother jumped out in the night.
That house is my first memory of wanting
not to cry,
of wanting everyone in the family to be all right,
but since they weren't—
of wanting to be a river.

GATHERING

When she went into the hen house
for the morning chore
the eggs were all sitting on the hens.
And the house was full of light
from the roof of the chicken house
being gone. Great morning gold
from the sky was warming the eggs
and the mothers were resting.

Maybe varmints are afraid
of coops without roofs,
because no one had been in through
the night—but all the great roosters
of the farm. They'd been in and
pranced up and down the dirt floor,
through the nests of straw.

You might as well say they'd been in
and pranced with razor blades
tied to their heels—
because it was impossible
to break any of those eggs
without baring a spot of blood.

PURE AND RAPID

The big dead tree burns
from the inside out.
The farmer filled it with kerosene
and now the chicken hawk and farmer
watch the fire. Chicken hawk
sitting on a new tree,
farmer standing close enough
to feel the heat the hawk
won't touch.
Hawk, farmer, neither
wish for gentleness
while they stare at the invisible
turned sharp shapes and colors.
The hawk thinks of the rough rust
coat of the heifer, the prize
that's too big for him
that he's certain is full of blood.
The farmer thinks of the room
above the strip-tease in town—
nothing in the room
but light from the neon tube
shining the walls red.

The air around the tree
knows the hawk and the farmer.
But like them, feels only the fire—
pure and rapid
radial pain.

SECRET COMMUNICATION

Remember when all the kids
sent off for those rings
they would touch in a certain way
while they silently moved their mouths
and someone else with that kind of ring
would get the message?
Same kids who sent off for the plastic
sheets they smoothed over the tv screen
and then used special crayons to make lines
on the show into words and meanings.
Never sent away for those things
at my house.
But I remember my phonics papers coming back
in first grade, a blur of red x's
wrong, wrong, wrong
and that tall old teacher, smiling
though really noticeably not sorry
that I didn't know what she was talking about.
Kids who miss school a lot
and then look out the window when they're there—
you can't teach them.
Same kids who miss the regular meanings
that the rest see
on a big screen, wear as easily as a ring.

I didn't like being that kid.
And I don't like the warm feeling I get
at the thought of having outlived
that tall white-haired teacher.

WINDOW

> *. . . character belongs to movement.*
> *Only the dead point is timeless.*
> —Paul Klee

The glass is baking in its frame
in the sun. This doesn't matter.
The sand has already been reduced
to substance even more timeless than itself.
Transparent, it is barely seen.

I look through the window for something important
to happen. But the endless cars in the street,
the ten or twelve children playing toy-gun games,
the spruce trees and nice houses
also become transparent.
The ability to choose the means
is my only comfort in the thought of death.
I look through all this
and imagine an erotic suicide pact.

        Two people are lying in bed.
They've done everything good
to each other that can be done.
They still need to know
what the other feels like,
how soft their lover is,
how hard their lover is.
They get to decide where to hold each other
as they start their slide into death.
I would like to be held with one hand
behind my head, in my hair.
I can't guess the place my lover
would like to be held.
The surprise would be part of the excitement.
Right now I would eat hot glass

if it got in the way of this fantasy.
Even the coming of Christ
hasn't stopped the world
from trying to keep the dead body from decay.

PASSION

I signed the letter, Mary
then noticed my mistake
and added: As you can see, I am going crazy,
I think I am a virgin.
Love, Mary.

There was nothing to feel guilty about,
it wasn't a bad letter.
I spoke some of my children,
a little of my husband.
While serious, it said nothing
about how serious I am.

No mention of the previous night
when seconds before I got into the car alone
I took a hammer and broke out
the windshield so life would be clear
as though through a clean windshield.

I wrote the letter as if worrying about God
mattered. I said, There's no sound
in my most immediate need: this air.
And there's also no desire.
But that's to consider
only one aspect. Don't forget the bitter
gesture of color—
no matter how many objects are struck by light
air is the same color when I see it:
silver not gold. My arms embrace air
the way my lungs embrace air.
I hold this stuff as if I need it.
But it could be water
I hold in my lungs

because as I know you've noticed
the air has no skin.
Holding it is like shouldering mirrors
in search of God.

Through the confusion I asked how her children were,
what had become of her husband
and how she systemized substance such as the breath
of those she loves.

It was a nice central letter
like one of those eggs
you put a small hole in each end of,
blow out the center and then decorate
for a religious holiday.

AND THEN

It was an old river town
and then the river moved away.
Happens all the time: the river decides
it doesn't like living next to people,
there's a flood upstream
and the river takes its chance.

The problem with this is that some people
who lived on the river
are now seriously grieved.
They do not like waking up
to a line of sand
where the day before they saw bronze water
waiting to silver itself with the moon.

These people may tell themselves
it was not very good anyway, living
with the river. Not as though
the river was even the same river
from hour to hour. Now that they think
about it, the only constant was the bed.
That and the knowledge that the sound
earth and water make when they touch
is something to sleep by.
The sand forever in the making.

WHEN I AWAKENED OUT OF MY HEAD

I had a glimpse. Now I think I know how
it happens—losing the mind.
I had a glimpse through
the iron swirls at the end of our bed.
You'd gone out. I'd gone to sleep
fearing a family could be killed
in its sleep, by you. When I awoke
I wasn't sure if you were in the room
straight ahead of me; the door was dark.
Light from the vanity
did not shine. There was nothing
to tell me where I was. The swirls in the bed
did not speak, the stairs to the children
did not speak. I recognized this place
but did not recognize this house.
I went past the time when one wakes up,
when one should know. I passed it looking back and forth
from right to left in the room
to find something I could focus on,
something I'd never loved.

All I could see was the air
that catches in your eyes when you look
out of bed after making love,
but this time, *it's fucking*.

Yes, the air is fucking.

WHAT WE DON'T UNDERSTAND ABOUT LIVING

I keep dreaming an explanation
of these stairs. Standing on the steps
I ask you to notice the rises are rock
chiseled from living rock.
You, still believing something you don't understand
might be explained by context,
ask me why I'm not afraid to pause on stone
that has endured
yet uttered nothing.

I look to the top of the stairway;
only clouds and blue sky.
Then I look to you and say:
In my dreams, we always understand.
In my dreams no one throws herself on the stairs
and puts a wet mouth to the stone.

WATCHING

In the yard next door are three news reporters,
two television cameras and a conservation officer.
This is life in a small town.
A young deer runs along inside the neighbor's fence.
The neighbor has just been photographed,
interviewed, and gone inside.

I've been trying to write about *us*—
I've already been out to watch the deer
as it jumped from our dog pen
to the yard next door.
I turn to the desk and pick up a paper
that says: Remember in the old house
when you took a crowbar
and pulled down that stretch of fence?

I was going to apply that fence, figuratively,
to our new sheets—the blue and white
striped cotton called "Pickets."
I was going to make myself think
about why we bought a new bed last year,
about why I spent so much money
on sheets and pillow slips and a comforter.
And then I saw this trapped deer
that had jumped in yet couldn't jump out.
But that deer doesn't remind me
of either one of us because that deer
is going to get away alive.
Even those sheets don't remind me of us:
they are strips of white fence
and strips of blue sky.
We live a relationship blind to such clarity.

DRY

The dead brush is stacked everywhere
ready to be lit off. Yellow and white
grass lifts away from the ground.
And the tethered black and white goat
stands on a pile of old tires.
As though the goat no longer drinks,
someone has overturned the stock tank.

It is awkward—admitting to needs
no one else will admit to, says the goat.

MY PARENTS

I'm falling asleep again without my parents' arms
around me. Because I'm no longer their child,
I ask a quarter of the people I meet
to put their arms around me. Some say no
and walk away; others become like a blanket
thrown off in fever.
These are complaints!

My accusation is (if I could I'd say it
in a way to bring them to their knees):
When I'm cold, I'm afraid.
When I'm warm, I'm afraid.

After my son's first nightmare
he climbed into my bed—
I teach this child and myself:
we hold each other tight so we won't die.

RURAL CHILDHOOD

Do you want me to show you where the dog licked me
in the dream? But now that the dream's over
the act's invisible,
like water flashing its image
only when it moves in the stream bed.

My cousin took me to the loft of the barn.
We walked to the back
then he pointed down three stories
to the mud where the sheep fell dead
after a night next to damp limestone
in the dark basement of the barn.
I wasn't supposed to be in the loft,
it was too high. As I looked down
at the dead sheep, I knew I would never return
to even the first floor of the barn.

Sometimes crazy-colored cats lived in the barn.
But even news of litters of kittens
nestled in the hay couldn't lure me.
The news was always mixed:
not all the kittens survived their birth.

I remember standing behind the gate to the house,
safely watching, enjoying watching
the sheep shearer working at the entrance to the barn.
But then, with the first sheep running naked
from the shearer, they came back to me
in the form of multicolored air—those mottled kittens
that didn't live to open their eyes,
those still sheep in the mud,
the dog smashed in the road with its tongue hanging out.

HOW LIFE CAME TO THE LAND

Say the sky is beached on the shore.
This means it finally happened
that where the sea and sky touched
became real
and the sky rode in
not so much to its death
but to a taste of sand
it would never have been tricked to
without the water.

COLD WIND

The wind lays its head on the house.
It makes so much noise waiting
to be let in I get up and open the door.
The invisible pulls at the wallpaper,
touches the curtains repeatedly.

With the door open I no longer understand
what the wind wants. Only that it cries
more easily now.

Be careful, I say to myself, It's music.

III

DEATH

The two people became so old
that the last time they sat down
at the table together they both
tucked the table top, rather than
napkins, under their chins.
When they stood up, they walked the table,
with great effort and wheezing,
down to the pond, grasped the top
from under their chins
and threw the table into the pond
like one throws a napkin onto a table
after an argument. In disgust.
The hermit came out of his turnip tree
next to the pond and said to the old people:
I saw a table running on all fours;
fruit fell from bowls, milk and wine sloshed
from cups just before it jumped
into the pond.
The old people shook their heads as they watched
the oak napkin stir silt: We didn't see that.
The hermit said, I lied,
the table wasn't running, it was walking, very slowly.
The old people shook their heads
and because the wind was chilling them,
they turned and walked back up the hill
to their house. The hermit returned to the twilight
inside the hollow of the turnip tree,
the turnip tree that sucks water from the pond
with straws as long as roots.

LUCAS CRANACH

I know what he's saying
when he titles his painting
The Madonna with the Bunch of Grapes
and the grapes are only secondary
to what the sad-faced madonna holds
on her lap.
          Such a naked son
for a woman to shelter. A Christ
as bald as the green fruit
he picks from his mother's hand
while she looks away. Not noticing
he holds a grape too close to his lips.

          A tease,
this picture of a baby
near to choking on the skin.
An artist saying, Don't laugh, don't laugh.
As he holds his sense of humor
just visible through the membrane.

WITH, WITHOUT

> *It might be lonelier*
> *Without the Loneliness—*
> —Emily Dickinson

Relationship, yes.
Pain-pleasure, the Dutch painter
who hung clothes and necklaces from the walls,
covered the walls with what could be filled
only by the human.
The same Rembrandt
who drew himself
alone
over and over.
Who drew Abraham speaking, Isaac
listening—everything there
but the words.
Loneliness, the artist sketching
his wife sleeping
with her own hand at her breast.

THE SHAWL PIN

If I wanted to kill God
I would start out early in the morning
from the country of my choice;
say Bolivia. Countries with high altitude
have an obvious advantage:
you're halfway there.
I would go during the rainy season,
taking no chloroquine tablets
so I could get the jump
on the deity. It would think It
had taken me by surprise, invaded
my blood. I would say, God,
I was so cold with your malaria
I couldn't part with my shawl
even when the fever made me throw it off
I kept it close enough
to find again, my shawl pin always in my hand
as now, when it is searching for your heart.
If only I could find your heart
you would know what I think of deities
who kill people with insects.

LIGHT PLUS PERSPECTIVE

>*He [Botticelli] was only a realist in his intention.*
>   —Yidio Yashiro

The way the moon shone through the window
we were able to roll in and out of light
while we made love. This light came to us
as pure white, it not so much revealed
our bodies as matched them.
Which the darkness could not do—
in it the physical lost dimension,
became a closing of the eyes.

The day before we had talked of
leaving each other forever.
So when in the night
he laid his head low on my body
and moaned sadly
I opened my eyes for the light to take me in
and the darkness to sustain me.

ALIVE

Remember that portrait by Carpaccio—
Young Knight in a Landscape in which
the young knight is surrounded
in the 15th century by surreal trees
that send out leaves on only a few branches
while lilies and irises lunge
at the knight's knees
and an ermine smells a violet next to a plant
on which is propped—for Christ's sake—a paper
that says, "die painfully rather than be sullied"?
The birds aren't flying upside down
but they might as well be in this picture
where the artist signs his name
to a piece of paper posted to a tree stump,
where the clear blue of the sky
yields to the faraway hills
and the jumbled land where a boy
whose armor outshines his flesh
stands looking at no one.
His sword is raised by hands so much larger in scale
than his small fine face, it's unlikely
young Francesco Maria sat for more
than a study of his head, after which
another model posed in the armor,
after which Carpaccio reread the motto.

FROM THE STUDIO

Would you like to paint a Crucifixion?
No.
What is the first color you would use?
I don't know.
Think of it, begin with strangers if you must—
then write me a note when you have a plan.

Dear Master,
I am ready. I have decided to use a camera—
and a pure white cat
for the Christ, because a cat also
can appear to have two arms and two legs.
I'll work at night so the sky
will be quite black. The cross
will be of glass—I know someone
who can turn fine holes in glass—
nails won't shatter it.
My only problem, I don't know how
to keep the cat from twisting
the length of time
the exposure requires.
Please leave me a note
if you have a plan.

Dear Antoine,
I know a doctor so skilled in hypnosis
even cats become calm.
It may survive the sitting.
Would that be all right?
Will your work be as good
if we spare the cat?

Dear Master,
I am not using brushes.
I'm so afraid I've resorted
to the camera.
Who cares if the animal lives.

FREEDOM

I'm past the point of thinking my life
is punishment for something I've done.
The only problem with nursing the dog
from my own breast
is first finding a corrupt veterinarian
to pull its teeth.
From the darkness of the room
my husband says, I'm the hungriest person
you know.
          I crawl on top of him and say, I still want you,
can't I have you?
The instinct is to not let go.

Later that day, remembering nothing of the darkness
in the afternoon in the bedroom,
my wish is to buy a convertible car
and roll it.

AFTER NATURE

Suppose I cut off my hand at the wrist.
If I use one hand to cut off the other
I am still faced with one hand
which will do little good and not enough bad.

I decided against doing anything
to my hand. I must keep it to buy snails
figs and garlic from the street vendors.

*

Remember Caravaggio's paintings of all those heads?
*Judith with the Head
of Holoferenes* c. 1607,
Judith with the Head of Holoferenes
c. 1605, *Judith with Holoferenes*
too early to guess.
They are consistent with my feeling of unending isolation.
The 1607 remains the most beautiful—
the shine still on the man's black hair.
Call it *Crowning with Thorns*,
call it *Flagellation*,
call it *David with the Head of Goliath*—
one light, one plane, no gradations.

*

This is my body you see,
the imperfection of the human,
the dirt on the flesh of the pilgrim's foot.

The 1605 Holoferenes would have been the year before,
the 1607 the year after
Caravaggio committed the homicide in Rome.

Then fled to a new town.
The entire body must be excised
from the air, the earth;
the shine left on.

LONG STEP INTO DARKNESS
decorated and made me
—Exekias

The way he's remembered:
in the sixth century before Christ
a man who was both painter and potter
loved to tell stories. Because he could
command lines into tight groups
in which even silhouettes kill
precisely, Western drawing sprang
from the sides of wine jars—
ivy from the hands of Dionysus.
Black grapes and black sails
of Exekias forced the call
for naturalism.
No more black-figures.
Even by an artist
with the humanity to twice
inscribe on a jar:
"Onetorides is handsome."
Especially by a storyteller
with a weakness for painting
on the sides of faces,
faces in profile,
eyes that look you directly in the eye.

MOTION

> *Our very meeting*
> *With each other*
> *Is an omen.*
> —Archilochos

In a world that decorates
walls with stone accomplishments
and deities. A world of stone wheels
with four spokes each,
each wheel a reminder
of outspread arms
and legs.

THE SILVER COIN

The cows once believed that if you stand in a pond
shaped like a circle
during the full moon
you'll die. That was everyone's first summer
and it finally got so hot
the animals decided to hire another cow
to go in the water. Just to be sure.
This was a cow nobody cared much about
from the dry farm next door.
She squeezed through the wires one evening
saying there was no need for pay—
death would be enough.

She stood in the pond all night.

Now, during a full moon, the pond fills with animals
waiting for death. They call their pleasure
the other side of the silver coin.